ENDURING WISDOM

SAYINGS FROM NATIVE AMERICANS

Selected by VIRGINIA DRIVING HAWK SNEVE

With paintings by SYNTHIA SAINT JAMES

HOLIDAY HOUSE / New York

For John Briggs,
whose suggestion became this book
V. D. H. S.

For Henrietta Talbird, my mother,
and all my native ancestors…with love
S. S. J.

Text copyright © 2003 by Virginia Driving Hawk Sneve

Illustrations copyright © 2003 by Synthia Saint James

All rights reserved

Printed in the United States of America

www.holidayhouse.com

First Edition

Library of Congress Cataloging-in-Publication Data

Enduring wisdom: sayings from Native Americans /

selected by Virginia Driving Hawk Sneve; with art by Synthia Saint James.

p. cm.

Includes bibliographical references.

Summary: A collection of quotations from American Indians

throughout the continent dated from the earliest contact

with Europeans to contemporary tribal persons.

ISBN 0-8234-1455-8

1. Indian philosophy—North America—Juvenile literature.

2. Indians of North America—Quotations—Juvenile literature.

[1. Indian philosophy—North America. 2. Indians of North America—

Quotations.] I. Sneve, Virginia Driving Hawk. II Saint James, Synthia, ill.

E98.P5 E53 2003

970'.00497—dc21   98-038527

CONTENTS

Author's Note

There are thousands of "wise" sayings attributed to Native Americans, who had no written language until long after white people were well established in America. The quotations used here were spoken in prayer, in song, in orations, or in conversations. This oral tradition passed the culture through the generations. It was kept in the minds and memories of the people. White missionaries, historians, and many, many anthropologists translated—and sometimes interpreted—these songs, prayers, and speeches so that the words were also preserved in writing. Because the quotations were translated over many centuries, the style, grammar, and punctuation may seem odd by today's standards.

I want the reader to know that these sayings came from real people, and that I did not make them up to use in this book. In the End Notes the reader can see where I found the original selections.

Native Americans still believe that the earth is Mother of all. She provides food, clothing, and shelter for all people. The sacredness of all things is still recognized. When survival depended on hunting, fishing, and gathering, it was necessary to apologize to an animal for having to kill it or to a plant for harvesting it. It had to be done so that human families could live.

Native Americans were courageous fighters, and they fought for specific purposes: to acquire needed hunting grounds and then to defend that land. Most of all, the men and women fought to protect their families and themselves. If at all possible, the tribes preferred peace.

Religion was not a separate part of tribal life. Everyday acts were filled with spiritual meaning, and special ceremonies were held to make contact with the Great Spirit.

The Native Americans' lifestyle was totally disrupted by the arrival of the white people. The Native Americans did not understand the white ways, and they resented having to become like the whites.

Yet the wisdom of the past is still vital today. I have tried to show this by using passages ranging from Native Americans who made the earliest contact with Europeans up through contemporary tribal people who value their heritage. I noted the year of the original quotes, but found that some were so ancient at the time of translation as to have no date.

Virginia Driving Hawk Sneve

MOTHER EARTH

The earth is mother to all creatures,
On, within, and above.
We are all related.
Whatever one does,
Or what happens to another,
Touches all.

We, and our children,
need the chance to walk the sacred earth,
this final abiding place of all that lives.
We must preserve our sacred places
 in order to know our place in time,
our reach to eternity.

1997, N. Scott Momaday,
Kiowa author

I am the Maker of heaven and earth,
the trees, lakes, rivers and all else.
I am the Maker of all mankind;
and because I love you, you must do my will.
The land on which you live
I have made for you and not for others.

1760, Pontiac, Ottawa chief,
repeating the words of the Maker of Life

Look at me, friend!
I come to ask for your dress,
For you have come to take pity on us;
For there is nothing
for which you cannot be used,
For you are really willing to give us your dress,
I come to beg you for this,
Long-Life make,
For I am going to make a basket
for lily roots out of you.
I pray you, friend, not to feel angry
On account of what I am going to do to you;
Take care, friend!

Ancient words of a Kwakiutl woman
to a young cedar tree before she took its bark

The bubbling water comes
from the rain cloud.
It represents the sky.
The meat stands for the four-legged creatures,
our animal brothers who gave themselves
so that we should live.
The steam is living breath.
It was water;
now it goes up to the sky,
becomes a cloud again.
These things are sacred.

1972, John Fire Lame Deer,
Sioux Medicine Man,
on a pot of good soup

I never kill a bird or other animal
without feeling bad inside.
All true hunters have that feeling
that prevents them from killing
for killing's sake.
There's no fun in just destroying life,
and the Great Spirit puts that shadow
in your heart
when you destroy his creatures.

1940, Joe Friday, Cree hunter

You ask me to plow the ground.
Shall I take a knife and
tear my mother's breast?
Then when I die
she will not take me to her bosom to rest.
You ask me to dig for stone.
Shall I dig under her skin for bones?
Then when I die
I can not enter her body to be born again.

1880s, Smohalla,
Nez Percé spiritual leader

THE PEOPLE

He was a hunter, warrior, and medicine man.
Strong for his family and band.
She sheltered, clothed, and fed her family,
Lovingly caring for all.
The young and strong learned from the old ones,
Whose wisdom guided us well.
Then strangers came to the land.

I am a fox, I am supposed to die.
Whatever is dangerous, let me do it.
1880s, Tokala, Lakota,
Kit Fox warrior society song

You speak to me of dangers
that I may fear,
but I have willed to go, my friends.
1800s, Osage warrior

You see, we *have* power.
Men have to dream to get power
from the spirits.
But we *have* power—children.

1936, Marie Chona, Papago woman

Open your ears and listen to me.
I have always taught you not to lie.
I have always taught you that a liar
is not worthy of being considered
a man.

1729, Stung Arm,
Nachez mother
of the young chief Sun

Brother, our ancestors
considered it a great offence
to reject the counsels of their women.
They were esteemed the mistresses of the soil.
Who, said our forefathers,
bring us into being?

1788, Good Peter, Oneida chief at a grand council,
speaking on the importance of including women

Guard your tongue in youth,
and in age you may mature a thought
that will be of service to your people.

1860, Wabashaw, Dakota chief

It was our belief that the love of possessions
is a weakness to be overcome.
Therefore the child must early learn
the beauty of generosity.

1911, Ohiyesa, Santee physician and author

You must speak straight so that your words
may go as sunlight to our hearts.

1871, Cochise, Apache chief,
discussing a peace settlement
with the whites

Let me be a free man—free to travel,
free to stop, free to work,
free to trade where I choose,
free to choose my own teachers,
free to follow the religion of my fathers,
free to talk and think and act for myself—
and I will obey every law,
or submit to the penalty.

1870s, Joseph, Nez Percé chief,
who unsuccessfully tried to lead his people
to Canada to avoid moving to a reservation

WAR AND PEACE

Fiercely I fought for my land,
When I could not be left in peace.

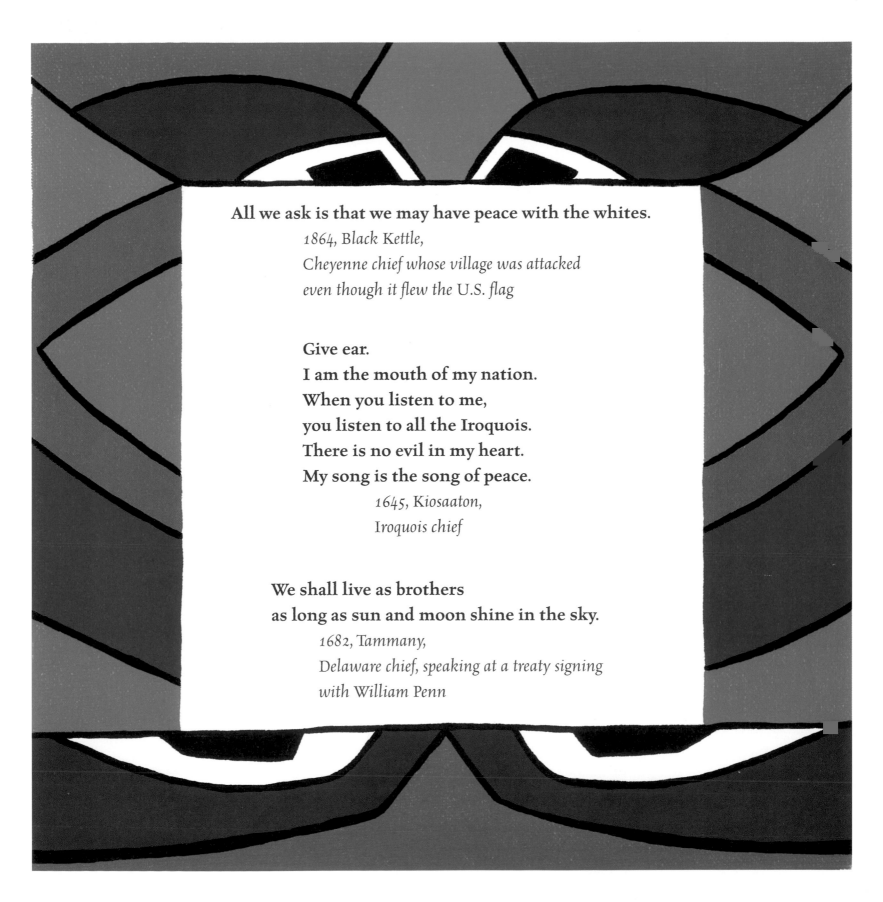

All we ask is that we may have peace with the whites.
1864, Black Kettle,
Cheyenne chief whose village was attacked
even though it flew the U.S. flag

Give ear.
I am the mouth of my nation.
When you listen to me,
you listen to all the Iroquois.
There is no evil in my heart.
My song is the song of peace.
1645, Kiosaaton,
Iroquois chief

We shall live as brothers
as long as sun and moon shine in the sky.
1682, Tammany,
Delaware chief, speaking at a treaty signing
with William Penn

We think if the Great Spirit
had wished us to be like the whites,
he would have made us so.
We believe he would be
displeased with us
to try and make ourselves different
from what he thought good.

1829, Decori, Winnebago chief

What is civilization?
Its marks are a noble religion
and philosophy,
original arts, stirring music,
rich story and legend.
We had these.

*1927, Grand Council Fire
of American Indians,
memorandum to the mayor
of Chicago*

SPIRIT LIFE

Great Spirit,
Be with us in all that we do.
In all of our days.
We'll live the best way we can
And not be afraid
Of life's end.

We also have a religion
which was given to our forefathers,
and has been handed down to us,
their children.
It teaches us to be thankful
for all the favors we received,
to love each other,
and to be united.

1830, Red Jacket, Seneca chief

I had learned a great lesson
and now knew that the ceremonies
handed down by our fathers
mean life and security,
both now and hereafter.

1940, Talayesva, Hopi,
as an old man remembering
his youth

We were profoundly religious,
believing that the world existed
in a precarious balance
and that only right or correct actions
kept it from tumbling.
Wrong actions
could disturb the balance.

1993, Wilma Mankiller,
former principal chief
of the Cherokee Nation

Things may be going well
for you one day,
then something happens
and you are destroyed.
This is the way life is.
Remember, it can happen
to you, too.

Ancient Diequeno mourning song

Do not grieve.
Misfortunes will happen
to the wisest and best of men.
Death will come and
always out of season.

1818, Big Elk, Omaha,
when an old man

Out of my childhood memories and dreams and meditations,
also from the wisdom of the old people,
the ones who knew the old ways, comes a spirit of love and tenderness
that the Eskimo needs to give to the world.

1962, William Willoya, Eskimo, telling of his dream

ENDURING WISDOM

We live on reservations.
And in cities and towns across America.
Some of us are poor in possessions,
Others have more.
We work with our hands and our minds.
We grow food, build houses, dance, and sing.
We're sportsmen, doctors, and teachers.
We make the laws of the land
And fight to protect it.
We value our heritage and can learn
From its enduring wisdom.

If all of us
and all living things
on the planet are to continue,
we, who still remember
how we must live,
must join together.

1996, Leslie Marmon Silko,
Laguna Pueblo author

We are also products of a rich and ancient culture
which supersedes and makes bearable
any oppressions we are forced to bear.
We believe in tribalism,
we believe that tribalism
is what has caused us to endure.

*1961, National Indian Youth
Conference policy statement*

We try to teach our Indian children,
do not be ashamed,
even though you are Indians.
Think like Indians, be like Indians,
but learn English,
learn how to write,
be educated.
You have two minds
and you can work with both.
We do not want to lose out
on being Indians.

*1967, Buffalo Tiger,
Miccosukee leader*

It is our Desire that we and you
should be as of one Heart,
one Mind, and one Body,
thus becoming one People,
entertaining a mutual Love
and Regard for each other,
to be preserved firm and entire,
not only between you and us,
but between your Children and our Children,
to all succeeding Generations.

1736, Kanickhungo,
Six Nations leader, at a treaty with the whites

We must continue to do good throughout our lives.
If we have corn and meat,
and know of a family that have none,
we divide with them.

1830, Black Hawk, Sauk chief, who led his people
to resist the whites in what has become
known as the Black Hawk War, 1831–32

People shouldn't be afraid
to learn about other people
and other cultures.

1996, Tatewin Means,
Dakota high school student,
on her award as a teen leader

END NOTES

p. 5   Virginia Driving Hawk Sneve.

p. 6   N. Scott Momaday, *The Man Made of Words* (New York: St. Martin's Press, 1997), p. 117.

Francis Parkman, *The Conspiracy of Pontiac* (New York: Collier Books, 1962), p. 224.

p. 8   Franz Boas, *The Ethnology of the Kwakiutl: 35th Annual Report* (Washington, D.C.: Bureau of American Ethnology, 1921), p. 619.

p. 9   John Fire Lame Deer and Richard Erdoes, *Lame Deer Seeker of Visions: The Life of a Sioux Medicine Man* (New York: Simon & Schuster, 1972), p. 96.

p. 10   Ellsworth Jaeger, *Woodsmoke: The Book of Outdoor Lore* (New York: Macmillan Co., 1953), p. 66.

Herbert J. Spinden, "The Nez Percé Indians," *Memoirs*, vol. 2, pt. 3 (Lancaster: The American Anthropological Assoc., 1908), p. 261.

p. 11   Virginia Driving Hawk Sneve.

p. 12   Leonard Crow Dog and Richard Erdoes, *Crow Dog: Four Generations of Sioux Medicine Men* (New York: HarperCollins, 1995), p. 8.

Francis LaFlesch, *The War Ceremony and Peace Ceremony of the Osage Indians*, Bulletin 101 (Washington, D.C.: Bureau of Ethnology, 1939), p. 31.

p. 14   Ruth Underhill, "The Autobiography of a Papago Woman," *Memoirs*, vol. 46 (Lancaster: The American Anthropological Assoc., 1936), pp. 22–23.

John Reinhold Foster, *Travels Through Louisiana* (London: T. D. Davies, 1771), p. 58.

p. 15   *Iroquois Women: An Anthology*, ed. W. G. Spittal (Ontario, Canada: Irocrafts Ltd., 1990), pp. 43–44.

p. 17   Charles Alexander Eastman, *The Soul of the Indian: An Interpretation* (Boston, New York: Houghton Mifflin, 1911), p. 99.

Charles Alexander Eastman, *The Soul of the Indian: An Interpretation* (New York: Houghton Mifflin, 1911), p. 99.

p. 18   A. N. Ellis, "Recollections of an Interview with Cochise," Kansas State Historical Collections, vol. XIII, 1913–14, pp. 391–92.

Chief Joseph, "An Indian's Views of Indian Affairs," *North American Review*, vol. CXXVIII, 1879, p. 429.

p. 19   Virginia Driving Hawk Sneve.

p. 21   Martin F. Schmitt and Dee Brown, *The Fighting Indians of the West* (New York: Charles Scribner's Sons, 1948), p. 43.

Frances Parkman, *The Jesuits of North America* (Boston: Little, Brown & Co., 1886), pp. 384–85.

Cavalcade of America, ed. Carl Carmer (New York: Lothrop, Lee & Shepard Co., 1956), p. 24.

p. 22   Rupert Costo, *Textbooks and the American Indian* (San Francisco: American Indian Historical Society, 1970), p. 140.

Henry Raymond Hamilton, *The Epic of Chicago* (Chicago: A. C. McClurg Co., 1906), p. 27.

p. 23   Virginia Driving Hawk Sneve.

p. 24   *American Indian Prose and Poetry*, ed. Margot Astrov (New York: Capricorn Books, 1962), p. 163.

American Indian Prose and Poetry, ed. Margot Astrov (New York: Capricorn Books, 1962), p. 248.

p. 25   Wilma Mankiller and Michael Wallis, *Mankiller: A Chief and Her People* (New York: St. Martin's Press, 1993), p. 181.

Florence Shipek, *The Autobiography of Delfina Cuero* (Morongo Indian Reservation: Malki Museum Press, 1970), p. 15.

p. 26   Addison Erwin Sheldon, *History and Stories of Nebraska* (Lincoln: The University Publishing Co., 1919), p. 46.

William Willoya and Vinson Brown, *Warriors of the Rainbow* (Healdsburg, Calif.: Naturegraph Co., 1962), p. 65.

p. 27   Virginia Driving Hawk Sneve.

p. 28   *Reclaiming the Vision: Native Voices for the Eighth Generation*, ed. Lee Francis and James Bruchac (Greenfield, N.Y.: Greenfield Review Press, 1996), p. 7.

p. 29   U.S. Congress, 90th, 1st sess., Senate Committee on Labor and Public Welfare, Special Subcommittee on Indian Education, Hearings, Dec. 14–15, 1967, pt. 1, p. 182.

Wilma Mankiller and Michael Wallis, *Mankiller: A Chief and Her People* (New York: St. Martin's Press, 1993), p. 20.

p. 30   *Indian Treaties Printed by Benjamin Franklin, 1736–1762*, ed. Julian P. Boyd (Philadelphia: Historical Society of Pennsylvania, 1938), p. 7.

American Indian Prose and Poetry, ed. Margot Astrov (New York: Capricorn Books, 1962), p. 140.

p. 31   Erin Anderson, "NEA Awards to Two from City," *Rapid City Journal*, May 31, 1996, p. 1.

7
453